Golf
Rules and Penalties

Like Never Before

By
Del Bergin

Copyright © 2025 by Del Lewis Bergin
All rights reserved.

No part of this publication may be reproduced, stored in a retrieval system, or transmitted in any form or by any means—electronic, mechanical, photocopying, recording, or otherwise—without the prior written permission of the author/publisher, except in the case of brief quotations used in reviews or articles.

ISBN
Paperback: 978-1-917327-86-2

This book is a work of fiction. Names, characters, places, and incidents are either the product of the author's imagination or used fictitiously. Any resemblance to actual persons, living or dead, or real events is purely coincidental.

Self- Published by Del Lewis Bergin
Printed in USA
First Edition

To my granddaughter, Alexandria Scurlock. She has filled my life with joy and wonderful memories. Her dedication, hard work, and passion for becoming a nurse continue to inspire me every day.

Acknowledgment

I would like to acknowledge my late brother, Denny, who was my golf partner for many years. We grew up together in Spokane, Washington, and shared countless rounds on nearly every golf course in the area. His memory lives on in every swing.

About the Author

I was born and raised in Spokane, Washington, and earned my degree from Gonzaga University. Shortly after graduation, I was drafted into the U.S. Army, where I served for two years. After completing a series of evaluations, I was assigned to the Pentagon with secret clearance, where I worked on programming the mainframe computer.

Following my military service, I married the girl next door — and we've been happily married ever since. The skills I gained during my time in the Army paved the way for a fulfilling career in information technology.

I'm also a proud twin and have remained close with my sister throughout the years. Today, I live in Texas, where I relocated to be closer to my granddaughter. Life continues to be a journey filled with love, learning, and family

Introduction

In these uncertain times, when debts and problems grow in direct proportion to duodenal ulcers and fatty tissue around the midsection, more and more people are finding relief from their daily tension—as well as a way to maintain that girlish figure—by taking up the game of golf.

The purpose of this booklet is to highlight some of the rules of golf and golfing etiquette by following two weekend golfers (using the term loosely) through nine holes of good-naturedly abusing the game.

Del: "That wasn't a half-bad drive I made—it was all bad. Just 100 yards, right next to that tree."

A single following: "I think he should play with a marshmallow. He'd get the same distance, and they're cheaper."

Denny: "You'd be better off driving another one from the tee and lying 2."

(Is Denny right or wrong?)

WRONG

Del could drop two club lengths from the tree, no nearer the hole, and lie 2.

If he elected to hit another drive from the tee, he would lie 3 wherever his second drive came to rest.

His original drive — 1

Penalty stroke — 1

His second drive — 1

Where his second drive landed, he would lie 3

It would probably be to Del's advantage, therefore, to play his first ball and not lose the 100 yards of distance.

Overshadowing Your Opponent

Denny: "I can't say that I'm a Happy Hooker, but that wasn't a bad shot for coming out of a fairway bunker."

Del: "Not bad, but I think you just hit my ball."

Denny: "Now, what do I do?"

Waiting single: "Asking him for golf advice is like asking Kojak what Hot Comb works the best."

Del: "That's ok. We'll just play the correct balls in the rest of the way."

   (Is Del right? Is everything A-OK?)

½ RIGHT, ½ WRONG

Del is right that no penalty is incurred against Denny since the wrong ball was hit from a bunker.

However, he is wrong in saying they can just continue playing—the rules require Del's ball to be replaced as close as possible to where it was originally before being mistakenly hit.

If the ball had not been in a bunker, Denny would have lost the hole in match play. In stroke play, he would have received a two-stroke penalty.

Note: Always check your ball before striking it, even if you're sure it's right where yours should be.

Bird Watching Instead of Ball Watching

Del: "I finally make a decent shot, and a bag gets in my way—and I don't mean my wife."

Denny: "Sorry about that, I guess that's the breaks of the game."

The impatient single: "These guys make this the only 480-yard par 3 in the world."

(Did Del get an unlucky break?)

NO

The breaks of the game are that Denny suffers the loss of the hole since he is in match play (by hole).

In stroke play, it would have been a 'rub of the green,' and the ball would be played where it lies.

If Del had hit his own bag, he would have lost the hole in match play or received a 2-stroke penalty in stroke play.

Note: Watch where you put your equipment—it could be costly.

Denny: "Great! I hit my famous straight ball on my second shot, straight out of bounds."

The frustrated single: "With his aim, I wish I were playing in front of him instead of behind him. He should be picked up for assault with a deadly weapon."

Del: "I guess you'll have to drop a ball where you went out of bounds and lie 3."

(Is Del entirely correct?)

NO

The penalty for out of bounds is **stroke and distance**. Denny would have to drop a ball where he stood and lie 3.

His shot from the tee — 1

His second shot, which went out of bounds (thereby losing the distance) — 1

Penalty stroke — 1

From where he stood, he would lie 3

Note: This same ruling applies to a lost ball. Denny would lie 3 from where he had hit his second shot.

Scoring Can Be Frustrating

Del: "This rough is so high, I'm lucky I didn't lose my ball. I'll have to press this tall grass down around the ball so I can get a good swing."

The single still following: "If he wants a good swing, he'd better try Sears & Roebuck."

Denny: "You should bend that branch back so you can get a shot at the pin." (Denny's leading by 3.)

(Are either Del or Denny suggesting anything contrary to USGA rules?)

Yes, Both Are Wrong

If a ball is in long grass, bushes, or similar conditions, only as much of the grass or bushes can be moved as is necessary to find and identify the ball. If Del tries to improve his lie, he would be subject to the loss of the hole in match play or a two-stroke penalty in stroke play.

If Del were to take Denny's advice and bend the branch back, he would be subject to the same penalty.

The lie or the line of play cannot be improved by breaking, bending, or moving anything fixed or growing. Exceptions are:

(1) If it occurs while taking a normal stance.

(2) If it occurs while making a stroke at the ball.

Additionally, the club may be grounded lightly but not pressed.

Note: You are not necessarily entitled to see the ball while attempting to strike it.

Straight-Lining It to the Next Tee

Denny: "One more slice and I'll have a loaf. Now I know why they call this a 3-wood—odds are 3 to 1 you'll hit it into the woods. I'll have to take a stroke penalty and take my ball back in the line of flight to drop it in order to get a shot at the pin."

Still persistent single: "With his slice, if he aims at the pin, he'd better watch the back of his head."

Del: "I hate to be the one to have to tell you, but I don't believe there is a 'line of flight' ruling."

(Is Del right? No line of flight?)

RIGHT

The ball cannot be dropped anywhere along the 'line of flight.' If the 2-club-length rule cannot be applied effectively, the only other option open to the golfer is to drop the ball behind the point where it lies, keeping that point between himself and the hole, with no limit as to how far behind that point the ball may be dropped.

In the example below, the ball must be dropped somewhere along Line B, not Line A.

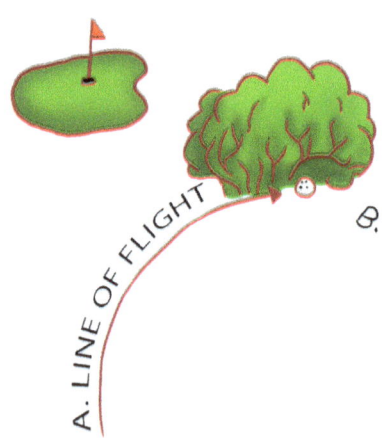

Note: If the ball is in a bunker and deemed unplayable, it must be dropped within the bunker.

Sand Castling

Del: "There, that ought to help—I put on my bowling wrist support."

The single again: "Believe me, nothing would help. He'd probably do just as well if he used the bowling ball too."

Denny: "The $0.10 a hole we're playing for isn't influencing me, but I don't think you can use that."

(Is Denny right?)

RIGHT

Any artificial device that might assist a player in making a stroke is prohibited.

A plain glove may be used, but a wrist support like the one Del is trying to use is a breach of this rule.

Del better remove it immediately, as the penalty is disqualification!

A Clean Ball Can Give You an Advantage

Denny: "Better watch the pin—I don't want to be penalized when I chip this into the hole. First, I think I'll remove this loose impediment from my spherical projectile." (Removes some grass from his ball—Denny's practicing his vocabulary.)

The single (about to become violent): "He has more loose than an impediment."

Del: "You can't remove anything from your ball until you get on the green."

(Is anything wrong in this situation?)

YES

First of all, Denny doesn't have to worry about the pin since he is not on the green. If he were on the green and hit the flagstick, he would receive a 2-stroke penalty in stroke play or lose the hole in match play. In this case, Denny has the option of leaving the flagstick in, having it attended, or having it removed. However, if the flagstick is attended, he may not strike it—if he does, he incurs the same penalty as if he were on the green.

As for Denny removing loose impediments—grass or soil that is adhered to the ball is not considered a loose impediment. Loose impediments are natural objects that are not fixed, growing, or adhered to the ball, such as loose rocks, twigs, leaves, and even insects.

A player may pick up and clean their ball only when on the green.

Note: Sand and loose soil are considered loose impediments only on the putting surface.

Lining Up Your Opponent's Putt

Del: "That shot was 200% perfect. I hit your ball farther away from the hole, and my ball ended up a lot closer than it would have been if it hadn't hit yours. I might get a good score on this hole."

Single (relieved that after 3 hours and 45 minutes of playing, he sees the 9th green):

"These turkeys think pars are something that grow on fruit trees."

Denny: "I guess there's no penalty against you, but I'm going to put my ball back where it was."

(Can Denny replace his ball? Does Del receive a penalty stroke?)

YES, NO

Since Denny's ball is on the green but Del's is not, no penalty is incurred.

Denny has the option of either replacing his ball or leaving it. Before Del took his shot, he could have requested that Denny mark his ball or putt out.

In stroke play, if Denny believed his ball might aid Del's shot, he could have marked it.

Note: If both balls had been on the green and Del had hit Denny's ball, Denny would still have the option of replacing it, but in stroke play, Del would incur a 2-stroke penalty.

Yelling FORE Can Be Advantageous as Well as Safe

Del: "Maybe we should ask this single behind us to join us on the back nine."

Denny: "Yeah, maybe we can hustle him into a money game."

Del & Denny: "Would you like to join us?"

The weary single: "I don't think so. I can see a storm coming. Besides, I only play nine—or for four hours, whichever comes first."

When Golf Becomes 'Russian Roulette'

If you are one of those golfers who insist on finishing a round no matter the conditions or potential dangers, keep in mind the mistakes Del and Denny are making during an electrical storm:

1. If you can't take shelter in a building (preferably steel-framed), find a low area. Never stay on top of a hill.

2. Never seek shelter under a lone tree.

3. Don't raise an umbrella or golf club until the lightning has fully subsided.

4. Avoid standing near a sprinkler system.

Remember, golfers:

When you may not be straight or far, And you may so seldom see a par, You might cuss and say, "I give up!" But that next shot might drop in the cup.

www.ingramcontent.com/pod-product-compliance
Lightning Source LLC
Chambersburg PA
CBHW061226070526
44584CB00029B/4000